T0131952

Lilly Jammes and Ben Jammes

La Mosca Zumba

The Fly Buzzes

Copyright © 2018 Lilly Jammes and Ben Jammes.
Interior Graphics/Art Credit: Ben Jammes

All rights reserved. No part of this book may be used or reproduced by any means,
graphic, electronic, or mechanical, including photocopying, recording, taping or by
any information storage retrieval system without the written permission of the author
except in the case of brief quotations embodied in critical articles and reviews.

Archway Publishing books may be ordered through booksellers or by contacting:

Archway Publishing
1663 Liberty Drive
Bloomington, IN 47403
www.archwaypublishing.com
1 (888) 242–5904

Because of the dynamic nature of the Internet, any web addresses or links contained in
this book may have changed since publication and may no longer be valid. The views
expressed in this work are solely those of the author and do not necessarily reflect the
views of the publisher, and the publisher hereby disclaims any responsibility for them.

Any people depicted in stock imagery provided by Getty Images are models,
and such images are being used for illustrative purposes only.
Certain stock imagery © Getty Images.

ISBN: 978–1–4808–6693–5 (sc)
ISBN: 978–1–4808–6692–8 (hc)

Print information available on the last page.

Archway Publishing rev. date: 11/13/2018

Dedicado a nuestro Papá,
que hizo aprender
Español sea divertido.

Saltar

Sal

No **salta** en la **sala** con **sal**.

Don't JUMP in the living ROOM with salt.

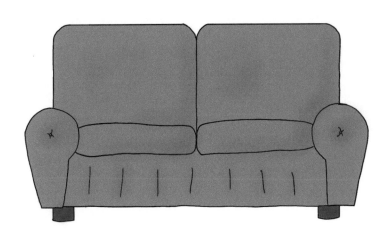

Hombre

Hombros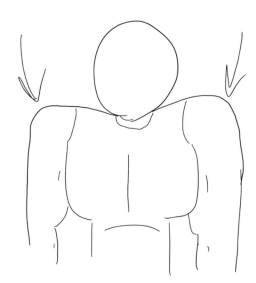

El hombre con los hombros tiene hambre.

The man with the shoulders is hungry.

Bruja

Sándwich

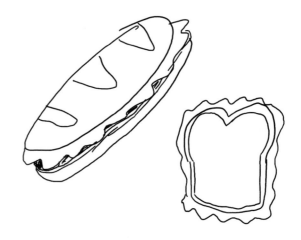

¿Cual bRuja tiene el sándwich?

Which witch has the sandwich?

Vaca

Vaso

La vaca verde ve un vaso de vino viejo.

The green cow sees a
glass of old wine.

Parar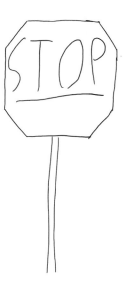

Pirata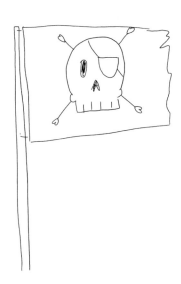

¡Párate, Piratas!

StoP, PiRates!

Papá

Pato

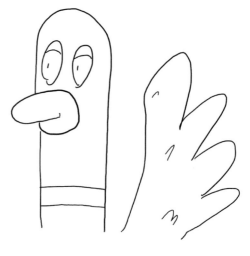

La **Patata** del **Pato** no es la **PaPa** de **PaPá**.

The duck's Potato is not Dad's Potato.

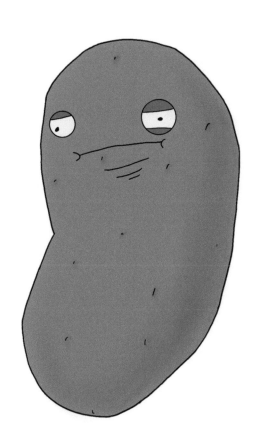

Hormiga

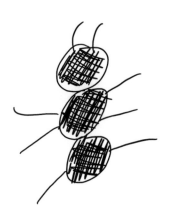

Horno

Las zanahorias horribles de la **hoRMiga** están en el **hoRno**.

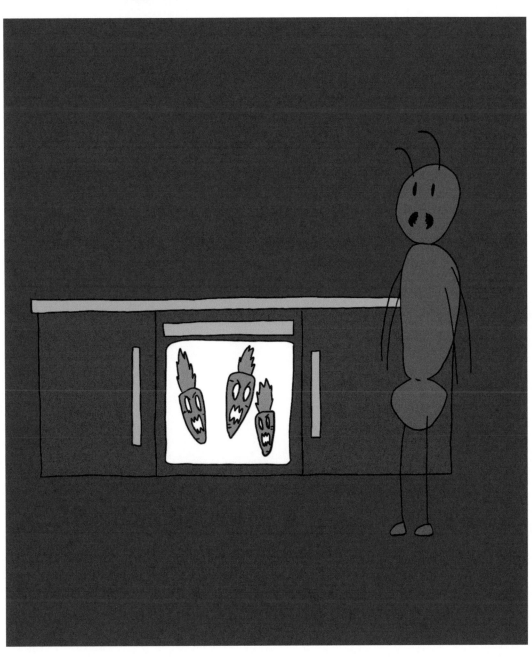

The ant's horrible carrots
are in the oven.

Mosca

¡La **mosca** zumba!

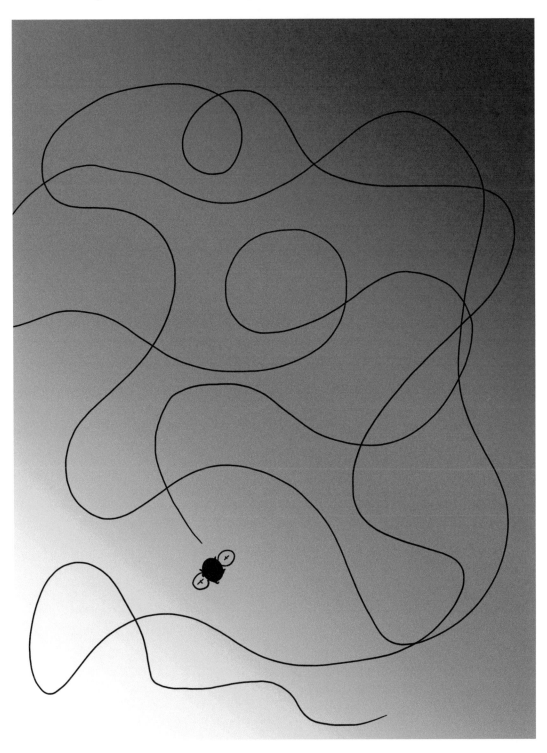

The **fly** buzzes!

Humo

Humor

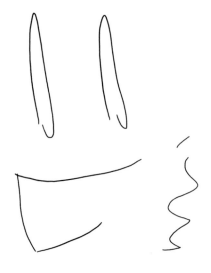

El **humo** del humidificador
no tiene **humor**.

The **smoke** from the humidifier

doesn't have **humor**.

Aseo /
Servicio

Ver

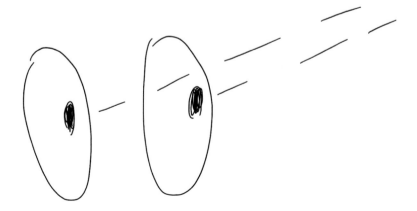

No veo el aseo del museo!

I don't SEE the
museum's bathROOM!

Lilly Jammes and **Ben Jammes** are a sister and brother duo who both speak Spanish as a second language. Lilly attends college at Tulane University in New Orleans, where she is studying music and architecture. Ben is a middle-school student who lives with his family in Seattle, Washington.

Printed in the United States
By Bookmasters